Stitch and Send

A fun and easy
embroidery-card kit for girls

illustrated by Jen Skelley

★ American Girl®

Published by American Girl Publishing

Copyright © 2013 by American Girl

Questions or comments? Call 1-800-845-0005, visit **americangirl.com,** or write to Customer Service, American Girl, 8400 Fairway Place, Middleton, WI 53562-0497.

Printed in China
13 14 15 16 17 18 19 20 LEO 10 9 8 7 6 5 4 3 2 1

All American Girl marks are trademarks of American Girl.

Editorial Development: Carrie Anton

Art Direction & Design: Gretchen Becker

Production: Tami Kepler, Judith Lary, Paula Moon, Kristi Tabrizi

Photography: Jeff Rockwell

Illustration: Jen Skelley

Craft Stylists: Carrie Anton and Gretchen Becker

Dear Reader,

Your greetings will be "sew" great with these ready-to-embroider folded cards. The holes are prepunched, so adding a pop of color and texture to each card is simple—just stitch along the printed pattern.

Start by learning lots of different embroidery stitches using the easy-to-follow step-by-step pictures and directions provided. Use the stitch-practice cards provided to try out the stitches. Then sew a card and personalize it with stickers to create a unique greeting card to send to someone special.

Your friends at American Girl

Card Folding

When looking at the front of the card, fold the right panel on vertical cards or the bottom panel on horizontal cards behind the stitched panel. Use double-stick tape to attach.

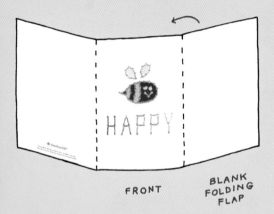

FRONT   BLANK FOLDING FLAP

BACK   FRONT

Supplies Inside

You'll find these items in your kit.

Cards (prepunched, blank, trifold)

Included in the kit are 16 cards—12 predesigned and prepunched cards and 4 blank cards on which you can create your own pictures and patterns. All of the cards have 3 prescored panels. The extra panel is used to hide the back of your stitches, which looks kind of messy. To the left are easy instructions showing how to fold the stitched cards.

Envelopes

Your kit contains 16 colored envelopes, one for each card. The envelopes are blank, allowing you to add cute doodles, the recipient's name, an address and stamp if mailing, or all of the above.

Safety Needle

The plastic needle included will prevent pricked fingers. A sharp point isn't needed because the predesigned cards come with the holes already made. Just thread the needle and start sewing!

Stickers

The embroidered stitches are the fantastic focus, but stickers help you personalize the greeting. For example, change a stitched card into a note of appreciation by simply adding a thank-you sticker. In addition to sticker words, cute picture stickers add a touch of pizzazz to your design.

Embroidery Floss

Use the 11-inch pieces of embroidery floss on the practice cards or to get your greeting cards started. Use your own floss to finish the designs and add more colors.

Practice Cards

Since some or all of the embroidery stitches included in this kit may be new to you, sample stitch cards have been included to let you practice before making the final product. Turn the page for helpful tips for using these cards.

Shopping List

You'll need some supplies not found in your kit when crafting your embroidered cards. These items are widely available, and floss can be found at most craft stores.

- tape
- scissors
- more embroidery floss
- pen

Sew-Cool Stitches

The following step-by-step instructions
will have you embroidering with ease!

Stitch Tips

Before you craft a finished card, use the stitch-practice cards to make sure you can successfully sew new stitches. Here are some tips:

1. Follow the stitch instructions in the book and on the practice card. Both will help you better understand the path your needle should follow.

2. To reuse your cards, leave a long tail when creating your first couple of stitches. The stitches will stay in place while you embroider, but you'll be able to remove them later.

3. Don't tug too hard when stitching. Even though the cards are meant to be reused, they can tear if you pull too hard between stitches.

4. When you've completed one card, carefully take out your stitches starting from the end and working back to the beginning. If you wish, practice again.

Stick Your Stitches

When sewing on fabric, you use a knot to keep your stitches from slipping through the material. When sewing your cards, use tape instead. You'll create a flatter surface behind the stitched design (a knot creates a lump). One small piece of tape on the back of a card holds the floss at the beginning of your stitching, and another secures the last stitch.

Embroidery Basics

These basic skills will get your stitches started.

RUNNING STITCH

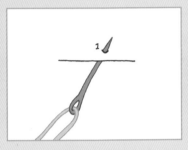

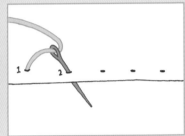

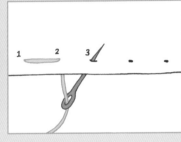

1. Starting at Hole 1, push the needle from the back of the card to the front of the card.

2. Send the needle down through Hole 2 to the back of the card.

3. Bring the needle through Hole 3 to the front of the card.

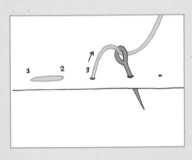

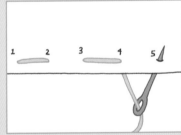

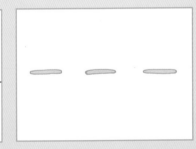

4. Repeat step 2 going through Hole 4.

5. Continue pushing the needle from front to back as shown in steps 1 through 4.

6. End the running stitch with the needle at the back of the card.

BACKSTITCH

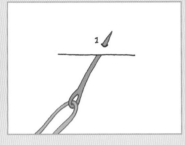

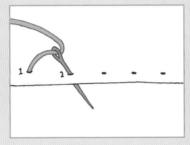

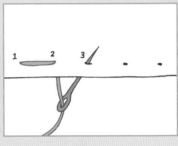

1. Starting at Hole 1, push the needle from the back of the card to the front of the card.

2. Send the needle down through Hole 2 to the back of the card.

3. Bring the needle through Hole 3 to the front of the card.

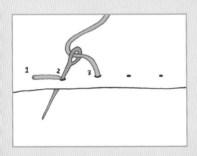

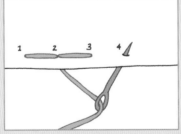

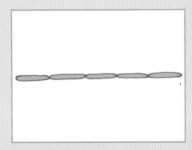

4. Push the needle back down through Hole 2.

5. Send the needle up through Hole 4.

6. Make more stitches by repeating the backstitch pattern in steps 3 through 5.

WHIPSTITCH

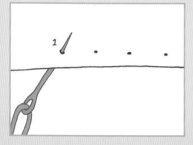 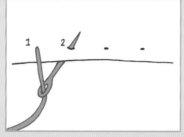 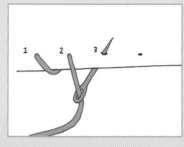

1. Starting at Hole 1, push the needle from the back of the card to the front of the card.

2. Wrapping around the edge, push the needle through Hole 2 from back to front.

3. Repeat step 2 through Hole 3.

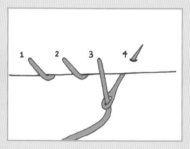 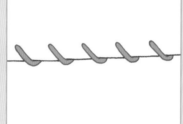

4. Continue pushing the needle from back to front as shown in steps 1 through 3.

5. Complete the whipstitch by taping the thread to the back of the card.

Practice your *Running Stitch*

Practice your *Backstitch*

Practice your *Whipstitch*

X Marks the Stitch

Follow these steps to give cross-stitch a go.

CROSS-STITCH

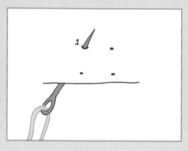

1. Starting at Hole 1, push the needle from the back of the card to the front of the card.

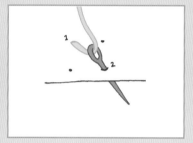

2. Send the needle down through Hole 2 and to the back of the card.

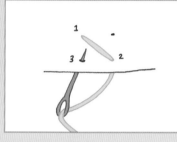

3. Bring the needle through Hole 3 to the front of the card.

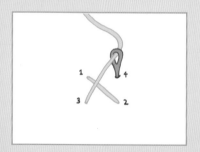

4. Push the needle down through Hole 4 and to the back of the card.

5. When making multiple Xs, be sure Stitch 1-2 stays below Stitch 3-4.

Practice your
Cross-Stitch

An Edge-y Stitch

See how the blanket stitch creates interesting edges!

BLANKET STITCH

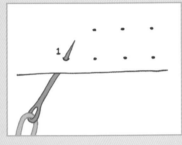

1. Starting at Hole 1, push the needle from the back of the card to the front of the card.

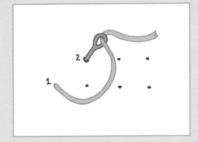

2. Send the needle through Hole 2 to the back, but don't pull the thread taut.

3. Push the needle up through Hole 3, now pulling thread taut to lock the stitch.

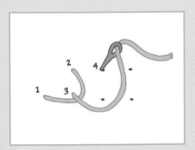

4. Repeat step 2 through Hole 4.

5. Repeat step 3 through Hole 5.

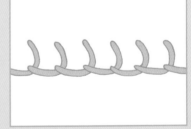

6. Continue in the pattern shown in steps 1 through 5.

Practice your
Blanket Stitch

Practice your
Blanket Stitch

Lovely Links

Interlocking stitches make an amazing chain.

CHAIN STITCH

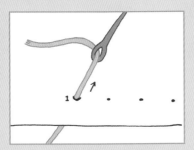

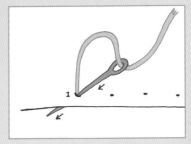

1. Starting at Hole 1, push the needle from the back of the card to the front of the card.

2. Pull up a small length of thread, making the start of a loop.

3. Start bringing the needle back down through Hole 1.

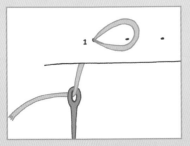

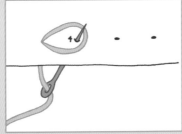

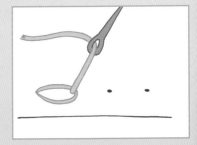

4. Pull the needle through, but leave the loop on top so that it wraps around the next hole.

5. Push the needle through Hole 2 to the front of the card, staying inside the loop you made.

6. Pull thread taut.

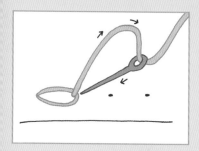
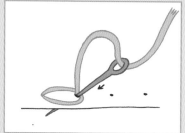
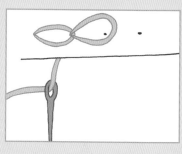

7. As in step 2, make the start of a second loop.

8. Start bringing the needle down through Hole 2, with the needle going inside the loop (not under it).

9. Repeat step 4.

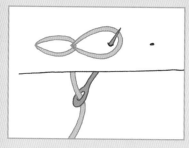
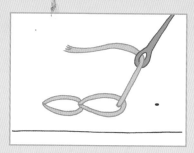
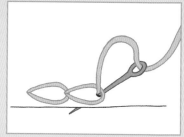

10. To end the chain stitch, repeat step 5 with a new hole.

11. Pull thread taut.

12. Push the needle down through the last hole, but on the other side of the loop, to lock the stitch.

Practice your
Chain Stitch

Practice your
Chain Stitch

ENDING A CONTINUING CHAIN STITCH

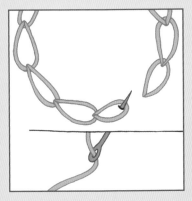

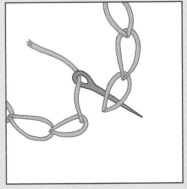

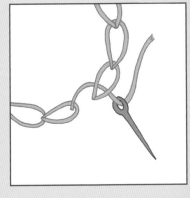

1. Follow Chain Stitch instructions 1–11 around a circular outline.

2. On the last stitch, slide the needle under the first stitch.

3. Pull the thread through.

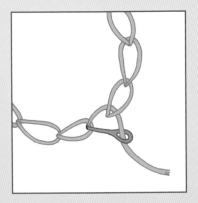

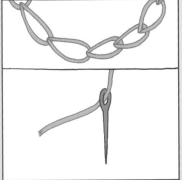

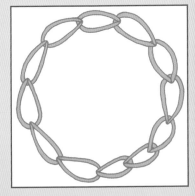

4. Send the needle back through the hole of the last stitch.

5. Pull the needle taut. Tape the stitch on the card back.

A Soaring Stitch

Use the fly stitch to give your embroidery a lift.

FLY STITCH

1. Starting at Hole 1, push the needle from the back of the card to the front of the card.

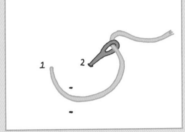

2. Pull up the thread, leaving a U-shaped loop. Send the needle through Hole 2.

3. Bring the needle up through Hole 3, now pulling thread taut to lock the stitch.

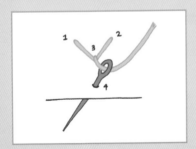

4. Push the needle down through Hole 4.

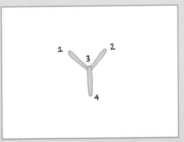

5. Complete the fly stitch by taping the thread to the back of the card.

Practice your
Fly Stitch

Twinkle, Twinkle Little Stitch

You'll be seeing stars when you follow these steps.

STAR STITCH

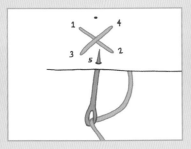

1. Complete steps 1 through 4 of the Cross-Stitch. Send the needle up through Hole 5.

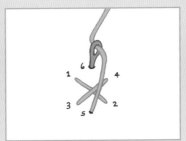

2. Push the needle down through Hole 6.

3. Tape the stitch behind the card, or continue if you want to make an 8-point star.

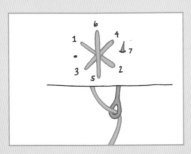

4. Bring the needle up through Hole 7.

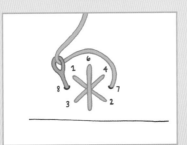

5. Push the needle down through Hole 8.

6. Tape the stitch behind the card.

Practice your
8-point Star Stitch

Practice your
6-point Star Stitch

Le Stitch

Add some French flair with this decorative knot.

FRENCH KNOT

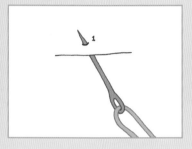

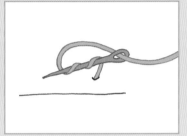

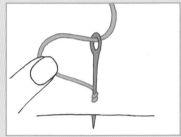

1. Starting at Hole 1, push the needle from the back of the card to the front of the card.

2. Wrap the thread around the end of your needle twice. Pull thread taut.

3. Use your thumb to hold the side loop created. Bring the wrapped needle back through Hole 1 to make a knot, letting go of the side loop as you complete the knot.

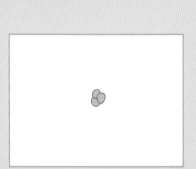

4. Tape the knot stitch behind the card.

Practice your
French Knot

Note
To make a bigger knot (or if your knot slips through the prepunched hole), wrap thread around the needle 3 or more times.

Card Creativity

Use these ideas to create cute and clever cards to give to friends and family.

Card Crafts

Turn your cards into clever crafts using these ideas:

- framed art
- a banner
- ornaments
- bookmarks

- gift tags
- paper quilt wall hanging
- place cards
- journal cover

- mini cards
- locker art
- small gift box
- scrapbook embellishments

The Right Words to Write

What do you write inside? Here are some ideas:

10 Great Reasons to Give a Card

Check this list if you're wondering why to send a card.

1. to say "happy birthday"
2. to say "feel better"
3. to say "good luck"
4. to say "way to go"
5. to say "I'm sorry"
6. to say "you're the greatest"
7. to say "wish you were here"
8. to say "thank you"
9. to say "hello"
10. just because!

Happy Birthday
"Many wishes for a special day!"
"May the best gift be this very day!"
"Each year you just keep getting better!"

Feel Better
"Get well soon!"
"I hope this card is your prescription to get better!"
"I'm thinking of you and hoping for a quick recovery!"

Good Luck
"I'm rooting for you and everything you do!"
"When you give it your best, you always win!"
"My fingers and toes are crossed for you!"

Way to Go

"Yay for you—you did it!"

"Congratulations for a job well done!"

"A big pat on the back from me to you!"

I'm Sorry

"I messed up. Please accept my apology."

"I'm thinking of you during these tough times."

"I'm sorry for your loss."

You're the Greatest

"I hope you know how awesome you are!"

"I look up to you and all that you do!"

"I couldn't ask for a better person in my life!"

Wish You Were Here

"Things just aren't the same without you around!"

"I'm sending you a hug from far away."

"Not a day goes by that I don't think of you."

Thank You

"Your gift brightened my day."

"I can't wait to show my gift to all my friends."

"Your gift is really going to help me!"

Hello

"Someone is thinking of you—me!"

"You make me smile every day!"

"Just a little note to say, 'Hey!'"

Be the Designer

With a paper punch and your imagination, create a card all your own.

Step 1: Pick a Theme

Use the ideas on the previous pages—or come up with one of your own—to figure out why you want to send someone a card.

Step 2: Sketch Ideas

Based on your theme, think of simple pictures you could draw that help show what you want to say. For example, draw a balloon for a birthday card, a four-leaf clover for a good-luck card, or a flower for an "I'm sorry" card. Remember to not make the picture too tricky to sew.

Step 3: Draw on Your Card

Using a pencil, lightly draw the picture you liked best from your sketches onto your card. If you make a mistake, erase and start again.

Step 4: Punch the Holes

Following the lines of your drawing, use a small-hole paper punch to make holes similar in size to those on the cards in your kit. Be careful not to make holes too close together, or you may end up with one big hole! If your paper punch can't reach the center of your card, draw your design in an area where the punch will reach.

Here are some other American Girl books you might like:

❑ I read it.

❑ I read it.

❑ I read it.

❑ I read it.

❑ I read it.

Discover online games, quizzes, activities,
and more at **americangirl.com/play**